X^n

By the same author:

Fishing in the Devonian

X^n

Carol Jenkins

PUNCHER & WATTMANN

First published in 2013
Published by Puncher and Wattmann
PO Box 441
Glebe NSW 2037

http://www.puncherandwattmann.com

puncherandwattmann@bigpond.com

National Library of Australia
Cataloguing-in-Publication entry:

Jenkins, Carol

X^n

ISBN   9781922186201 (paperback)
          9781922186218 (ebook)
          9781922186225 (kindle)

I. Title.

A821.3

Cover design by Matthew Holt

Printed by McPhersons Printing Group

This project has been assisted by the
Australian Government through the
Australia Council, its arts funding and
advisory body.

Contents

You

You do not know yet how often
I think of you, how I love
the way your hands pick up the book

and feel the smoothness of the paper
maybe you look around briefly
in case I am talking to someone else

but it is to your sweet face, your eyes,
so used to reading that you nearly
skim over the part I write about you

and that skinny kid who almost kissed you
and the way you lay in bed, the curtains pulled back
watching tendrils of stars curled

up there, listening to yourself think,
wondering about how time
might suddenly click forward

to what would come. Then you stop listening
to yourself think and hear the world hum.
Yes, it's you I am writing to.

How the Universe Begins

I

First it's a little out of focus, unformed
beyond a certain point of bunny rug
breast and bassinet. I invent all these—
and more— faces, baby talk, direct the film
of me on earth, write the textbooks as I read,
construct theorems to make space, stars,
nothing is too large to think into being
or too small to overlook once I turn
my mind that way, such as this pen
the poem and even you.

II

The great cosmic chicken fluffs, clucks
settles into serious cackling
and though some distance from her nest,
(that at that time does not exist)
lays an egg (here insert sound effects).

III

All this nonsense about a starting point,
assuming that nothing will produce something,
that the infinite must start somewhere, like yeah
whatever.

Night Facts

How Night Was Made

Once upon a time, before the earth
started to turn, people made lanterns
that gave off darkness
so they could sleep
but the lantern makers were careless
and left the dark lanterns out,
all together in one spot
making that side of the earth heavier,
and causing the planet to turn,
giving rise to nightfall.

How the Outside Works at Night

Only the lit parts exist. You will fall
into an abyss if you wander
into the dark.

Light or visions collect in places
of positive ions, forming a shield
which prevents the darkness
from seeping in.

Daylight is compressed by gravity
and lies exhausted, too weary
to move, shimmering faintly,
in odd corners of the sky.
This has been mistaken for stars.

Einstein's Overcoat

A Field Equation

Vintage, ninety five percent dark lining,
heavy, but not much to the eye,
over-sized, it bends all ideas of fashion
haloed by every garment it stands in front of.

Early on he tries to iron out its awkward angles,
slightly embarrassed that the label says 'Cosmological constant'.
For decades it is abandoned at the dry cleaners
but this coat never minds sleights of time.

Woven from a pure black bolt, slipperier than silk,
it runs and shies, a secret warp that threads
through Einstein, like doubt, with the quickest, finest needle,
the web and stain of a taut and universal fabric.

Return to Sender

You can be sure of death, and this:
every poet will make up, for what it's worth,
a poem on stars, starlight, nebula or red dwarfs.
But, mind the stars have got in first and made
the poet, ink, pen and page from spare parts,
with the caveat: *return to sender*.

Evolution by Engulfment

Is Darwin's something of a selective thesis?
(NB no complaints Charlie D)
his singular fix on the incremental
elements of evolution
for our well-bred step-wise
species— but like English
engulfing foreign words
we too shape shift by phagocytosis
imbibing and embedding
a welterweight of virus
a brio of bacteria.
Why, then, I ponder, when plants
got chloroplasts, did we stop
at mitochondria?

We are what we ate
(or myself with other animals)

Something of a zoo— that's me,
you too, with heists & thefts of DNA
from bugs, digestion delegated, eg *E. coli*
we're home base and an inland sea

genetically we're potpourri,
stomachs a doughnut hole
only seemingly internal
& blood a substrate for space invaders.

Co-evolution

The first eggs ever laid were covered in a fine pelt of nutrient fuzz which grew out of the many pores in the shells. The pelt kept the egg warm and acted as camouflage, allowing the Egg Layer to leave the egg to its own devices. The animal within the furred shell, known as an Eggling, would wind in the nutrient fuzz, eating it in a distinct pattern that identified both the animal and when it would emerge. This meant the Egg Layer could keep a watchful eye on its progress. Some of the more sophisticated Egglings invented a rudimentary alphabet writing their name, invariably with the suffix, or prefix 'Egg'.

The trouble with this evolutionary grandstanding was it taught egg collecting species how to read, putting these eggs at greater risk. Those Egg Layers and Egglings that did not quickly adapt to readers and drop the hair-o-grams with their overt declaration of edible contents became extinct. Evidence for this hirsute history can been seen in modern eggs which are covered with vestigial microscopic pores. If you examine them closely you will sometimes find the word 'egg' is still faintly patterned into the shell.

Waiting for a Name

for J & A's baby

You are as light is to the feather,
a body now given over to your own making
you're building you with milk and sleep,
air, the warmth of breath, a focal point.

Your triple O's are no emergency but a week, or two
at most, on your way through to the double O's, O's,
then integers starting with ones and twos.
You're watching, adding, as hands held tight

to sweat and fluff, uncurl to feel the world.
You are light and will learn our voices,
the rising tones, the gurgling gushes
as you're building you from words and sleep.

Your watching builds the cribbed world rib by rib,
as your crying might separate us from sleep. Sweeter
is your appetite for smiling faces, your sense that slows
your heart beat to match your makers'.

Bats, Botanic Gardens, 9 am

Hung body bags, en-leathered fur, animate
fruit talking in high frequencies;

unsettled, seething, the click of claw
and air slapped about by webbing. They sway,

dark cocoons set high in branches, their feet
commas in the grammar of inversion.

The smell of ammonia and fermented figs
wafts down with their waking squabbles.

Uneasy sleepers. We walk beneath, whispering
about how they've ruined these fine trees.

Sky Given

Bag-worn, begged case, borrowed by me
from the tree, fallen would-be tail
or possum body part,
a silk pillow case, stick wrought,
home spun, by the bag moth, Pyschidae.

Shroud and swaddling cloth,
camouflage, fashioned into fashion
identikit by its owner, eye tricker,
tree sticker. Meal ticket for a magpie.

Note: Pyschidae is the family name for the Bagworm moths.

In loco parentis

Sky claxon, sleep stealer, winging into any nest.
Pest. Egg bowler, orphan-layer, ruckus-maker
who crimps dawn's silence into shrieks and bar rests.

Interloper, striped insinuator, you're the nemesis
of decent nestlings, the betrayer of hapless hosts:
fig bird, oriole, honey-eater and Spangled Drongo.

Guilty party of the broken home, headache-er,
curse-originator, cause of canopy cacophony,
despicable delegator, cuckoo of another rule.

South Easterly

Frond hiss, ti-tree susurration
scarf ends tending horizontal
eye whites red with pollen itches

the bird bowl's load of water
a dimpling and rebounding
artefact of sky and leaves

curled leaf-eddy patterned
into court yard corners, grit ends
creeping under doors

the twist and reach, the fall
of shirts and sheets, fattening pillow
cases and empty dancing trousers

coats blown open, hair redone
pages turned to fluttered waste
skirts uplifted, petals blown

sky words stretched to meaning
-lessness, storied giants doff their heads
meringue clouds merengue west

Water under the Bridge

November, late afternoon, the lagoon
double-dinks its load of light and water
under Queenscliff Bridge, condensing
its tessellations where the current squeezes

round the pylons, it's travelling under, out,
digging greener beds and purling
round a brown and upright stick, over
the filamental green superannuated shells.

Then radiating around the canter-
lopping, high-stepping setter that circles
in his feathered wet and prancing joy,
it slides east, past the shadow

of the bridge, nips out the inlet's
quicker deeper breach into the surf,
laps the feet of the man who zips
himself into a Short Tom, kicks out

as salt spray across the face of waves,
it paves a gully ramp for the kite-boarder,
runs sweetly in dispersing ways.

Perianthetical Apple, Cherry, Plum

Tree petticoats, false lingerie, winged flotsam,
fall to me, sift and shake, and bus the breeze,

lay petalline on beds of gardens, float pink
and white from cherry trees, collect, dispel,

disperse, deceive, stay on, lie down;
maybe your fall perturbs me?

Set out in fives and threes, your pose
as clustered perianth is disposed by puffery.

Be flower wrap, pollen pot, carpel king,
tepal tide, bee bait and wasp impersonator,

house of plum state, modified leaf palace that duples
into picnics, prints, pillow words and porcelain,

sometimes cover of stigma, style and anther,
for *Malus domestica, Prunus serrula, Prunus mume,*

you are glory, gobsmack, gregal, descending grace-note
and colour grid, giddy girasole bending sunlight,

an acrobat of gravity and air, a blow-in,
you blouse, disrobing beauty queen
and everything between, play petal mist for me.

Young Ted Hughes' Jacket

– from his *Poetry in the Making,* Chpt 1, Capturing Animals

At threshing time his jacket seethed,
the lining lined with sixty mice
he conjured from stooks
and sheafs. Their thin claws
ran the taffeta, their fine teeth incised out
the interfacing. Rising like boils,
they nested in the frayed inside
of the hem.
And when he set the jacket down— or free—
it shivered off on hidden feet,
pullulating with its smell of must,
ammonia and millet seed.

Paring

You were like this knife
I had cut myself on,

every time I saw you
the wound wanted you back.

Alprazolam

After three weeks dropping
down the dose curve, their pink
scored ellipse— a bitterness
that bites the tongue,
then melts to liquid blackness
to make the night's work
an easy run of sleep,
and eases off the ratchet
of daytime-angst— starts to taste
as good as gin, sweet like radicchio:
welcome home the tongue
says, do come in.

The Coach's Son

His eyes are pale as chlorinated water, though
the green tint has left his lank blond hair,
his shoulders to his waist are still some kind of mad

GI Joe ratio, built from two or three thousand
mornings of squad laps. The trophy phase —
where he was taken to the pump room for a beating

if he was slow. Now he's very slow
pulls out a block of hash thicker
than a lane marking, shaves off

a pleat and rolls oblivion. Later heroin,
dissolves him completely—
like Disprin in water.

A History of Fever

A too desperate gesture and my fickle ally
the thermometer, cooling its column in the fridge
shoots out from its sleeve to shatter
on the floor, collecting as it breaks,
the broken glass of other experiments—
falling test tubes and lab thermometers, Pyrex beakers,
the vacuum pump for spilt mercury,
and further back from 1A Science,
dear Mr Smith, rolling its silver quickness
in his palm. Guilty again, I sweep
up glass shards and mercury.

I tilt the ashpan so the beads rocket round,
attracted to each other but separate as
scenes from my own fevered history.
A certain panning collects them, but no matter
how I coax this biographic element— with angles,
passes— the beads will not coalesce, but race together
all one way, and flow back the other.

Zero —vs— Nothing

To describe the difference between zero
and nothing, say zero is a certain space
before she knew him, a space three feet
in front of her, with some air in it.
Then he arrives, a person to whom she assigns
the value of one. Their inter-personal distance
fluctuates between a long way off and 0.1 mm,
with a mean distance of one car seat.

In the equation which adds up how she likes his leading tone,
subtracts his dislike of dancing, is divided by his determination
that kissing is the square root of a negative number,
and then takes away the value of one she had ascribed to him—
including all phone calls and letters—
what is left is Nothing: a nothinglessness.
Even the air that had been in that space
three feet in front of her has been cancelled,
it's so nothing that she falls straight
into it, a cold space that nothing can illuminate.

Exit Speed

Let x be the speed of what you're doing,
to do something else you'll need $(x + y)$,
where y is your motivation to reach
exit speed: that power to divert

from a chair, the kitchen,
a boyfriend or a house
y's the quantum force to slip,
to extricate, to effect escape

from each habit's orbit and the orbit's habit.
The man that leaves his wife, the plane the runway,
moss spore the sporangia, all spend on speed.
The highway, made for leaving, sets
out the neat condition: Exit Speed

Set Pieces

In the set of things that are
all of the things not in the set

a poem might work best.

$$\pm \infty$$

In the set of things that must
be false to be true

the liar is a popular and honest choice.

$$\pm \infty$$

If a marriage, a Mr, Mrs set up
makes of a and b a singleton and

an ordered pair $(a, (a,b))$ is this fair?

$$\pm \infty$$

In the upset of things that are
sometimes for the best

probability is at odd times
super scripted [to a higher power].

$$\pm \infty$$

A disorderly pair approach a revolving

door, A says you go first, B says, no, you,

C queued behind, huffs O it doesn't matter.
How many times will the door rotate before C leaves?

$$\pm \infty$$

If where you are placed in space, is
an ordered triple, and your history
is the set of all these past spatial triples,

does the intersection of another's set
mean there are times when (a) you're not you,
(b) set expansions must contract (c) you're pregnant?

$$\pm \infty$$

Where there is a new relationship xRy and x exists such
that x has relationships with $z_1 z_2 z_3 z_4 \ldots$, this will establish

that both y has relationships with $z_1 z_2 z_3 z_4$ and z_1 etc have
relationships with y but only while xRy holds,
if xRy fails, $z_{etc} Ry$ must fail: this is the law of de-facto sets.

$$\pm \infty$$

Where all the players on Court 2 are members
of the club, but some are more highly strung,

is it a racket if the pair who through no
faults of their own, lose 1, 2 etc to the nth set?

$$\pm \infty$$

[Take squared root vegetables, chicken bones,
make a stock of it, strain, set the stock to run over
fresh squared root vegetables, chicken bones] y de capo

Strain liquid and time its set to jelly. Plot setting time x
against y to find the stock's cube.

$$\pm \infty$$

If the lights are down to black,
and there are no actors, song lists,
props or flats
is the set still in the set of sets?

Unit of Measurement

In his shirt pocket, he carries, with him,
quotidian, the card recording all shifts
in his weight with the date. This heart-close
data sets out the substance of him,
proving he has his own measure.

A Play on One String of La Carrodus

Or Monday lunch with R. Tognetti

Dark honey, from bees drunk on bouquets
from dead brides, thinned back with black vinegar,

> Fading light, six wretched blissful souls
> who cannot bear to be together or apart.

> Miss Seyfert speeds a line of silk through
> crêpe de Chine by the fine lance of her needle

> while the Contessa nearly ignores the trysting
> letter dropped, from her pocket to the floor.

A field of poppies loosed in their own dreams
three fish swimming upstream,

> Monsieur, Le Comte, up all night losing at Bezique
> assays the bloom on the Contessa's skin,

> then catalogues his debts, the interest,
> against his Mama's health and the vial of laudanum

> waiting in Herr Doktor's bag. Miss Seyfert
> stabs the needle deep into her finger.

A room of silver samovars folding steam
into guests who bow and sit down to tea.

> Herr Doktor shifts slightly in his chair
> watches a single bird cross the blue weight

of sky hung between the curtains. Slides a
patent shoe towards the uncollected letter.

A drop of blood swells itself, delays, then slides
un-remarked, to meet its predecessors on the carpet.

Monsieur Le Comte standing at the door turns over,
again, the kopek in his pocket.

The maid catches her new reflection
in the kitchen window. It won't let go.

Then the sound of glasses falling, one by one,
somewhere down the hall,

and petals singing, as they too float down,
in the orchard.

Book Ends

Assortments stolen and derived from N. Pounder's No.1 Catalogue

Hide Bound, Titled In Gilt

Where did Brennan get the goatskin?
Perhaps, parched, he swigs down
beer while driving, hits the gravel
shoulder, flies off into a paddock.
The goat's done for. Parchment?

says Brennan, while Lindsay's etching
all the details half red, half Moroccan
in his notebook. His pages numbered,
sans serif, CB radios ahead with annotations.

The Invisible Book

Tactile but subtle linen, an unpublished work
by Burroughs in his foolscap phase.
Transparent interleaving and no markings
whatsoever.
Somewhat bruised by inadvertent jostling.

Slessor's Copy of the Ferry Timetable

with Kenneth Slessor's ownership signature
in two inks, one blue-green, one watery. Some
underlining on weekends and public holidays.

My Self as Rare Edition

Oh, I've had my corners bumped
(NB. no drawings by Gary Shead)
hardbound 1st edition, small print run

(one). A fine copy in an illustrated
chiffon wrapper, bound by lemon
polka-dotted cloth, necessarily

scarce but un-foxed and un-Kippled.
Stab-bound but still talkative, inscribed
'poet's dummy' — no actual poems included.

Heart Felt

I was heart felt, felt
as in new slippers, underlay,
a fine black beret,
and when the hammer
blow of her valves
slammed, I insulated,
an insurance against susurrations,
murmurs, buffering the SOS

of dysrhythmia. In fact infarction
was my brief, through the thick or thin
of H, or L, density lipids, I was greasing
stringy *Chordae Tendineae,*
and when it all went camembert-shaped
in her central cloverleaf
I felt nothing but relief.

Leaving Town

Was it the down and outness of the fluorescent
half-dark in a bus station on the seedier side of town,
the pre-dawn passengers—

the single mother with two kids under five,
bleary-eyed hugging pillows, the older lady
with mid-blue leisure pants and matching top,

the girls in tight jeans and thongs
blowing puffs of white air that hung themselves,
cold ghosts before us all,

or maybe the bus engine turning over,
the slide and slap of the door
wheezing open like a smoker, edging aisle-wise

into a seat, where your glass window twin gazes
back at you, dawn spreading over the roofs
and wet tarmac, the city getting dragged off by the highway

your face blurred by unexpected tears,
an ache of loneliness for leaving
a town you never thought you liked that much,

or was it just going, gaining speed, a high view
of telegraph poles, houses giving way to hobby farms,
then real farms, stretching out forever.

Five Hour Country Drive

It's 450K of road kill, oat-coloured stubble,
'I ♥ Kate McHeath' signs,
ex-trees posing as dead wood,
spring lambs with their mothers,
paddock dams like pocket mirrors;
so hours after, in bed slipping off to sleep
I'm still in motion and the vibrato
of wheels crossing the corrugated
white line on the shoulder,
shudders through the car. Sleep's the creepy
hitcher I slowed but did not stop for,
but now he makes a one–eighty,
so here's my lift, the dream car, engine running,
and I'm already in it, at the wheel.

Recovery Rate

Driving round these suburban avenues,
I came one night to a roadwork tableau—
a machine hissing and trembling,
men in white overalls and fluorescent vests
holding long wands
and tamping down a fire that was burning
up from the road, they seemed to be
sealing up a hell set on escaping.

Serious, intent, they worked to put
that brilliant hot blue-centred yellow
back into the ground,
the way the man who burns the letters
of love and assignation from another's wife,
works casually and deliberately to smother
the print, the flames, even the smoke,
to douse all symptoms within, all signs without.

F3

Driving, I put up my anti-poem shield,
warding off poetic clouds— like Achilles,
like all the other drivers on the F3,
I turn my eyes aside from little billabongs
of road left stranded by improvements,
ignore the caverns of dark rocks
glistening with the mountain's tears,
the snake skin shreds of tyres by the edge,
and if I've told you clouds once I've told you
a metaphoric number of times, blow off, blow over,
I am refusing all beauty, all strangeness,
I am on the F3, the road more travelled.

You are Invited to A Party

For Mark Walmsley

Crepe paper crowns, askew as smiles,
a crooked paddock, under a grand acreage
of clouds, in red jumpers and dirt-knee-ed trousers,
they're all peering at us, through the aperture
of a Franke & Heidecke Rolleiflex TLR
squinting through their reversal into a negative,
past their first flurried printing on Kodachrome,
the feted days, or weeks, or years, of display,
then, patient, patient in the lens of albums;
surviving foxings, cullings,
revivified and more than inquisitive about us
as they travel now by pixel pony
along time's parabola
squizzing, smiling, through the screen
wondering who we might be
with our strangely familiar aged skins,
our creased eyes and various blemished
thickenings, they still stand, in survey of us,
foundling princes of tender curiosity.

Susceptible to Louvres

The louvres in their lazy semaphore
splice and resplice the phoenix palm, the fig,
the summer afternoon that hangs,
late and potent in the daze of sweltering heat.

Venetian in their pivot points, glass colludes
with light, refractive in its prismatic
edging. Each split suggests I live by freeze-
frame shift, as summer, weighted, is suspended—

but wait, I've succumbed to this effect before,
and recall: an afternoon tempered, woozy
with anticipation, a shuttered bedroom's
purl of gold and plain, light and dark, my reflection

naked in tribal stripes and sliced up views
of road, front fence and lawn, the great world
without, the hiss and sigh when you
pull the cord and shut it out.

Slipping and Sliding,
[or a brief Rock n Roll history of me]

The first word I danced was shoes, though later
I eschewed Patricia K's big sister's
Elvis blue suede poster as a creepy decrepitude.

Clack-clicking my Bata Click-Clacks
three girls and I choose which Beatle
each likes best, I say they must be wearing wigs
so convinced am I of the paradigm
of short-back-and-sides.

The kitchen radio ranges from Never on a Sunday
to Macarthur's melting Park, a crackling puzzle
of blue velvet pieces, the titles jigsawed into the charts.

At Terrigal Beach Jim rumbled, a tsunami
from the tiny door in the Surf Club speakers,
where his fire stalled my feet, sole deep
in the burning sand, trailing my parents,
with my favourite things— a blue fringed beach towel
and a crab-bag, across a weird and mystic land.

Apple green I buy my first 45, Ringo-ishly
like its B-side It's a Revolution best, but Hey,
years later before the Stones arrive at Randwick,
pulled by six white horses, a stadium—
with me in it sings, exultant, *I want to hold your hand.*

A sudden shift, a sandbar kind of drop, from radio
to homemade tapes, that arrived with biro'ed labels

I get to hang in Laurel Canyon, rest cassetted in Cripple Creek,
say Goodbye to Madame George and all sand-castle virtues.

The Abba summer of blackberry nip with the white fur
of lemonade, Saturday nights dancing in houses
absent of sense and parents, the fifteens— tipsy dancing
queens, while off-stage in the pass-out bedroom
my best friend vomits on the dry-cleaning—
a kind of purple Waterloo.

Argued they were wild, but they were wild wild
a noun of quick four feet, so pent up & iambic
while we sun-baked rotisserie style, puddles
of paddle pops in our too hot hands, high on the ebb tide,
and green grass of our wild wild courses.

Thrashing Max Laschenko's mother's Morris
1100, round the KFC car park, an impromptu
lesson in stripping gears, John Kay counsels
— very loud— *get the motor running,*
and explode into space, while the Morris bunny hops.

Light the candle, put the bodhisattva at the door,
no fools, about your clever work
you got our number, and Rikki's letter.
We were lushly crushed in your Muswellbrook debut
hey nineteen?

Every day for six weeks, I watch the clock, and at six
put Ten CC on the turntable and when I see him coming
up our drive, I lift the needle's arm, and set it to play
I'm not in love and don't forget it.
It was a silly phase I was going through.

In Clapham Place, free live to air
concerts at the Double JJ,
fifty people more or less
shove into a studio space.
I step over Wendy S., dosed flat
with smack in the Ladies,
who staggers up to torch two sets
floating on Wilbur's wild saxophonic cloud.

So much higher than all the stairs
I coast into the Horden; its twelve foot high
No Smoking signs convey nothing to me
the usher does though, so co-operatively I flick
an embered B&H off into middle distance
before shuffling up to take my front row seat
for Little Feat. It can't be beat.

In Brisbane Street, behind the Wentworth pub,
heading out for a dish of beef chow mein
in silk slacks and second hand pink cashmere,
I order Grand Dame champagne,
& what about a starter of that white cocaine?
Who drove a Goddess around the bend, well yahoo
we heard the radio play, yahoo, so much is so, is so, old school,
and who can never get enough at Lee Ho Fook's?

Once upon a time I had a habit
of coining my bric-a-brac lunchtime dollars
into the juke box at The Mac — and sighing — for John Lennon
filtering his jealous guy through Brian.
A slow boat later I see Mr Ferry re-do this dreaming
from the worst seat in the house
at the oxymoronic Entertainment Centre.
Live concerts get converted into tales told by videos.

Rehabed into the lyric mode, Mr Costello changes trains
to McManus, declaring in his wild haired mania
Noble's mere idea, that melts my knees
and every eye, and as we swing across all styles;
Elvis smiles.

Two weeks apart PJ Harvey and Nick Cave's
concerted efforts show a crowded demographic
difference, in Polly's I am in the 95th percentile
and in Cave's I am in bloom, as the jaded,
the acid-etched, the speed-fried & the soaks
get steered by their better halves to a tableau
near the bar, in leather jackets, dolly-healed,
for a refill at the Big Top, Luna Park.
The constant thrill of after dark.

To be continued...

the king of fakey

(aka Jeff Stockwell)

Glides backwards, speed being
cut out in milliseconds, the grain of paint
on handrails, his bearings quick
inside their wheels. Gravity gives up on him

having lost the argument with centrifugal
force, the noise runs a whirring ladder
that pirouettes, inverts & somersaults.

We see the gnarly cuts, clean moves, sweet
air, the brittle bouncings from moving gear,
mad drops, runs up the wall and then the king

stops, nudges back his taped together glasses,
smiles, a complicity I nearly can't believe.
Is it knowingness, being bashful or the angle?
Un-bladed is he plain, nearly solid & low on grace?

Cupidness

For years Cupid is my boss, sending me to stand
talking and fidgeting in bars, to lose concentration
in conversations. The dress standards she exacts

mean expensive underwear, legs groomed to silk
slickness so that each might fall for the other
as it tests for smooth. There are letters of demand

to write, journal notes— part game-plan, part fieldwork,
late night taxis to take, windows to stare out of
on rainy nights and sentry duty in phone boxes.

Then almost I think I'm fired, slipped off the payroll,
unemployed, no more night shift, no more stupid bar work
but then I find, here I am again, doing this.

Breaking, Glazing

His was first, hers was second,
two broken panes of their own doing.

Both were doors, his front,
hers French. He used his fist.

As he was absurdly drunk,
on instinct she follows his hand with hers,

then lifts and reverses his hand safely out,
his wrist's blue veins still sealed.

For hers, she was in that fervent
kind of biting misery and took

aim at him, with everything
on her bedside stack of crates.

A slight twist and most things missed him;
it was the cut-glass lid of a dish,

(one of a pair— she would not miss it)
traversing the bedroom's giddy air

that de-crystallised along with
the French door's upper half.

First he, then she, re-glazed their handy work,
measuring up, pulling the old pane out

with snapping pliers and chiselling off
stiff crumbs of ancient paint-flecked putty.

Then tapping in the holding tacks, as piquant-sharp
as make-up kisses, the awkward placement

of that transparent, dividing sheet,
the oily smell of newness in the putty.

His has a hair-line crack in one corner.
Hers is whole but falls just short of fitting.

Climate is what you expect;
weather is what you get.

If weather is the watch, then climate is the calendar

Who stole my tartan biscuit tin?
He frowns, and clutching the front door,
declares to the cleaner,
My first wife was beautiful, now I have her;
a shrew, a witch.

In her nightie, his one and only
wife, shrugs, Ah
The first wife, she says,
I knew her a little too.

    A husband is what you expect,
    marriage is what you get
    while anniversaries, school fees,
    mortgages and bills accrue.

House of Barometric Pressure

She had the raincoat years,
in and out of that strange faux
Swiss chalet— while he knew
only sunshine. How did they cope?
Still, never a cross word.

Cold front

Yes, they married early, she left
(bloody cow, he said, other blokes
from the start). If it was your kidneys
that didn't work you'd see someone,
she said, angry still, years after far
too many knock-backs.

Mares tails and mackerel scales

Worse than cooking tripe was Club Cricket.
She prayed Friday nights for mackerel
skies and rain. Nothing avails; their youngest
wasting Saturday afternoons,
watching the TV test pattern.

Earth system modelling program

Their orbit, Friday night
fish and chips early, then a single
dinner waiting, cold. Time sticking on
the clock like araldite,
the fight forecast for ten minutes
past a slammed car door.

Saturday morning arrives
with burnt toast, a squall of words
and Bex at breakfast, offset by hot moist
troughs of laundry, the humidity
of sat'day matinees.

a high pressure belt in the mid-latitudes

Clothes tightening up like airline pressure stockings?
Try degassing the mid-latitudes, cut out butter
week night wine and soft cheese.

hectopascals

The unit of hectic pressure
small children can exert on
a single female when all are penned
indoors by weather.

active low pressure system

Tazos, yugio cards,
War Hammer, X-box, Assassins Creed,
COD, One Piece manga, laptop:
always the horizon of purchase
which I am gently worked towards.

orographic ascent

We could not agree when
to leave, the mountains were slow clapping
like thunder, mocking, knowing. By the time we get
to the pass the rain has lost all discontinuity:
visibility is the bonnet plus three feet.

> *A marriage is what you expect,*
> *a husband is what you get.*

Infidels

Slipping past my many sentinels,
I am, say, melting butter for béchamel,
or falling into sleep, into the tease
of the lovely mellow slide of molten yellow,
or the sheet warm, feet warm
abandonment of all anxieties,
when an insight, an understanding, wraps
its strong right arm around my waist
we size each other up and smile,
god I love you I say to this strange notion,
with that whole of body love
that turns all the cogs and gears
of arms and legs, we intertwine ten
fingers like we invent decimals.
Our feet are binary, bodies primary,
all the steps lead to an answer
so wholly writ we have no need to speak,
no need to reflect or replay,
to be in this time and know
is sweet as fresh cut grass.

Hand Wash Only

Dear thing, come here, so your fine weight
lies warm and waiting in my hands. Let me correct

the small travails of wear, the spots and sweat,
the sags and stretchings. Here, let me hold you under,

drown your love-in-the mist merino
of mousseline translucency, so your sleeves,

and chest, your just-right v-neck submerge
in warm and fragrant suds, I'll squeeze you firmly,

before the towel blots out the rinsings,
gently re-shape your body for the hereafter,

and I swear I won't betray you with dark loads,
hot machine washes or the dryer;

and please don't listen to those old knitteds
whispering, liar liar liar.

Skeined

Starting out, your double-twisted, soft fall of silk
undoes like Rapunzel's plait, a cascade of thought-soft
threads; then the debacle of where to start, that loose
end hidden but – snip! impatience sets me off

and borrowing two other hands as posts I progress
in my unravelling till I've got a small tight ball of silk
and a tangle that craves attention. I set the skein
before me & worry off more thread. Things get worse.

It's gridlocked, a dreadlock of entwined falling in,
around & over. Knots with a polynomial power,
chaos with no budge about it. Ruefully I take the scissors
to excise snarl from skein: each cut will be a knot

I will not want. I make scant headway then put the skein
and the tangle's maze aside for daylight.
Next morning, proceeding with its silk circle laid before me,
I wind off thread that floats on no more than a flex—

as though the skein wants to find its way into a ball.
Errant ends are re-united in three balls of yarn
but the nub of disarray, a dishevelment remains,
a puzzle to un-make: a hex.

Conversations in My Bedroom

words from the ensuite mirror

Don't come too close, at this stage
of life we're both short-sighted
and I prefer you a little off, like ripe cheese.
I am dealing with soap film, ambience, dancing vectors,
reflections and refractions from that rotating glinter
the gully's weather vane, and god knows
you look fine to me just where you are...

song of the bedroom dust

We are the dust, or dusts or dustings, the once-were-floating
motes, in part you, in part cotton and some things that we're
not so sure about. We aggregate in films and eddies,
to spell out time, netting hair and dander,
pulvilio for finger prints until your soft caress
with a singlet still warm from your breast
recollects us for the wash.

china nags: ivory scolds

We, the boudoir ornaments, antique pieces & tasteful
modern classics, with provenance, are a little bored,
Madam, with your of-late lack of witty tableaux;
neglecting us for mere words and ink.
We know you click and pose on paper.
Be warned: laser toner has little depth,
and the silverfish you feed no metale.

shoe; shoe

We have each other? Well, yes and no. Odd times,
she's boxed us in but mostly, lazy, left us
in 'dissed pairs, shoved under the chaise,
to loaf or talk in tongues. Soles come and go, some
boast of foreign parts, others lament puddles,
the runners stutter about sand.

If once or twice, late at night, frustrated, my
partner is left out and loiters in a tripping way
on her path between bed and bathroom,
I won't say it's not right.

the chaise

Cut to, me? Me? Oh, drowned most days
or more precisely nights, in the hollow
ghosts they wear, ghosts that vanish
then reappear, and then she folds
and smooths them into the drawers.

I am a kind of open storage system
a portmanteau that never walks.
Still, I still have those rare moments,
late afternoon, when she curls up,
with a book for us to read, that
soft white quilt to keep
us warm. Yes, sometimes my eyes
are closed but I'm just resting.

Book Club

For Vivian Smith

I cut it fine, ten minutes house to ferry
someone's car reverses, I swerve in,
slam the door and sprint.

On the ferry, surprised to see you
most convivial of local friends,
you've seen my run, my breathless moment,
yours is the quiet watch of everything. I am tempted
to breach protocol and hug you.

We ensconce in talk of books,
the loveliness of Caspar David Friedrich's
clouds at the NGA, Absent Knowledge,
the French café in the Rocks,
one instant I look at a man behind us,
who's reading what's left of a book—
covers gone, edges rotten, spine guttered,
pages yellow-browned and thick with damp.

Like a razor, he slivers in,
nearly beautiful in his homeless apparition;
matted hair, scent of mould, mordant gaze
fixed on a rotting page
too real a ghost to be imagined
a man intent but barely visible
behind us whose homes are rich with books
and in ourselves a surfeit of text.

You say later, this is a poem?
I say yes. You cut it fine, the ferry pulls in,
the water laps. Your friend sits,
starboard, reading something rotten.

Post

Galileo says people are like paper;
would I dispense with 'are' or 'like'?

Last life I was a silverfish
this time I took to ink,

and when the post floats in
with a letter, an elegant sketch,

simple paper, complex idea, Oh I
praise reading's merit, to deliver

an afterlife, a parallel, a re-incarnation
a vicarious sense of being someone &

somewhere else, in the here and now
while holding nothing but cellulose

perhaps a gram of ink, a slip of graphite,
a lined page, headed 'Dear Carol'.

'As the light stays on to fade'

As the light stays on to fade, I climb the stairs, gain
the chaise lounge. Resting with a book, the pages close.
Under a soft and antique quilt, my left foot becomes kindle
to the right as I watch the scene outside grow more intense.
Three stills— a phoenix palm with shadow herringboned,
a paper-bark with currawong, the third, a plain
& darkening indigo— are all framed & spliced by the blinds.

A Cartesian impulse suggests this interstice of half-light & dark
might begin as well as end the day, that time's singular direction
is a convention too much praised. You and the children
silk in, to read and doze. We congregate. The colour's leaching
slowly from the trees, with bird notes scattering like bread crumbs.
Is this how families are meant to nest and slip off days like overcoats?

Surrender comes with twenty different speeds

The first fast hit is misleading, it gives only itches,
an impulse to speak, the inclination to spend three minutes
more than average, then surrender, sweet and unheeding.

Second and third, a tumble of eyes and lashes
that jolting instant of the blink,
a brink, easy to think the double-think.

Four are skirmishes of trespass or argument
you give up the inhibition not to argue
you roll your eyes, click or sigh and brush

your hand too close to the other cheek, a precipice
of proximity— you are happy more and more to
give up the six inches of warm air that envelopes

each. Fifth is the happy fall of no long term consequence
— except most can't get to six— the sex
disturbs them or if they do, it's an end in itself.

Seven is your lucky number, you give of time
and something milder— a taste for bluegrass,
a penchant for lakes and milk-white sheets.

The slow eight eats into your habits
you take up foreign sports or caraway seed
cheese, acquire a taste for smoky lapsang tea

not quite to please, you find a rationale
for certain genialities. Then comes a long
chain of gear ratio-ed concessions concerning homes

and mortgages and kids— that blur past like clothes
on the spin cycle— your investments are in decades
and filialities, now there is no point in counting.

Arguments become not quite set pieces,
and you find, it might be better to give way
as winning is merely another form of losing.

Sleeping becomes a serial distraction
You are jointly sensitized to third parties.
The past gains its own momentum

that interlocks, with your tangled washes;
loving the luxury of borrowed socks
and rites of passages read aloud as flowers.

The still nights waking to gaze at the beauty
of the sleeping husband, taking in
all twenty drowsy states' totting up of time.

The Shape of Water

Why do they still come to this last inch of water,
claws pivoting the bowl's rim
to dip further, further into the mixture tainted
with flecks of undigested fruit and seeds,
with its history of wind set out in leaves?

Rosellas, magpies, currawongs know this blue bowl,
the surety of its glaze, know its reflections
of sky and cloud and wind,
its surface tremolo from the beat of wings,
and these moments when there is so little in it
but it is water still,
know by faith the shape that water comes in,
and return as lovers to it again, again,
through emptiness and dregs and re-fillings.

Translated into Ten Languages

Looking straight into her eyes,
I shrug, shift my weight, right to left
drop to my haunches, smoothing the fine
short fur on the cartilage hind side of her ear,
making a small sound like a low-down hum
in my chest. It does the trick in dog,
or so she kindly let's me think.

Filling, leaving and refilling the same ikebana bowl
with water for three years on the deck rail,
whistling occasionally a few notes, carefully cleaning
off the sooty slime lining, so blue glaze + water
approximately equals sky, bath, cistern,
mirror, seismograph, the poem is now seven
dialects of bird, which might translate back to English.

The croupier plays Scrabble: the chips are down
in their roulette-a-thon, an acrostic
take on all the ball bearing's bets, red and black blurs,
the bounce translates into your pulse rate.

The string tail trails a fluid script, the sudden
side-ways shifts annotate discontinuities in tense,
the kite's translating wind, and I am reading
and writing in slow motion.

A History of Burnt Toast

"Smoke come, smoke come" Phillip Jenkins 1962

The cindered corner, smouldering in its slot
— the middle slice of three, tapered dangerously—
chuffs out smoke that wants to wend a way
to the alarm. Pop. The three bounce up
in another episode of the History of Burnt Toast;

smoke come, smoke come

In this history lemming-like the slices line up, first
the tank loaf's roundels, to bask
on the toaster's flip down sides, or stick singeing
to the wires. Who was watching?
No-one it seems;

smoke come, smoke come

Some slices never made it over.
Others, burnt, fuelled the arcane art
of scrapping, the grinding off of carbonised
ex-bread, embedding powdered cinders
forever in the butter. For hours the air is hung
with damp and sooty ghosts.
Smoke stains the cupboard's under-storey.
Then luxury: the orange Sunbeam Pop-up
with dial-in light or dark, that coined the term
'give 'em crumpet'. Still, nothing's perfect;

smoke come, smoke come.

The years when the first offering
to the Gas God was the fine hairs
on my fingers as the match flame met,
at last, the sweet stink of gas and a baffled
voomp of blue roiled out across the griller.
The bread's set out on old foil in a field of crumbs
while I watch its progress,
the logarithmic rate preceding thus,
not done, not done, not done, distraction;

smoke come, smoke come.

Then the invention of burning's aural amplifier,
the smoke detective, so as the raisin toast
—a risky item— fangs fast along the path to char,
the Dallas fruit loaf snaps its poppy seeds,
the sticky glaze of the French raisin bread
turns toffee hot and spiteful as they succumb
and smoke come, smoke come,
the detector screams in key you've come
to hate worse than charcoal;

smoke come, smoke come, smoke come.

Museum of Butter

Cork, Ireland

Notes: On what was there
and later thoughts on butter words

Butter milk and clabbered cream
butter ringers, butter tables,
butter paddles, butter papers,

butter boxes, butter stamps,
butter creams from butteries
buerre blancs and butter pats,

butter fingers, buttered paws
and witches turned to thieve
as butterflies.

Butter my heart: the museum in me

Left carotid, right vena cava
The lovely long length of the femoral
smeared and smothered with lipids' ease-ful
saturations, by this sweet food,
fine fatty matrix and taste conveyor:
a slippery ship of savour.

Staging a tongue load of easy rhymers

'Oh flutter it! I wish this banter
was something I could utter
without the cluttering
of stuttering' sighs Cho-Cho-San
sans character, tempted
as she is to dip into the lexicon
of the gutter. But then in any
adaptation is Butterfly's ex heart-twister
any better than a scuttle butt?"

Butter, Butter and More Butter
(Escoffier on being asked his secret)

Laid on cold and thick— so the teeth
dentate the paste, it smooths the lips

and our daily bread. The god of butter
the frying pan, the golden sizzle,

the batter lying, spreading
across butter's browning lubrication.

In butter-tics even bread
takes sides with butter

Saucy, coquettish in hollandaise
béarnaise, ghee and glazing,

the stave of pastry flakes,
the stuff of cakes.

Butter in its chemistry

Cheerful anti-oxidant
a solid that melts
to grease, the cheek of your
suspenseful emulsion

churned to break a whey
from your cream substrate.
For the careful, you're reversible
to your creamy infant state.

Reducing the green world to what is made

Butter: gold coined from a mammal world,
let down from bovine bosoms.

By argot: milkers, maids and buckets
pails, skimmers, dippers, creamers,
keeners, dashers, table churns
a milky linguistic of butter ingots.

By the buttering of my thumbs
all things superstitious come

Use a dead man's hand to stir
the milk and so make sure
the breaking. Another rule demands
all guests and residents to lend a hand,
to take a turn of the churn
for good butter and good luck.

A dairy man hurls a butter lump
into a pond, a river or a lake,
and cattle for the sake
of their good health are driven
into these buttered waters.

Fossil Butter

Iron Aged lumps of it found wrapped
in bark, tree trunks and odd leather skins.
Lardered in a fen's cold store
for lean times and for pilfering.
Were they laced with incantations?
Racinated, cloved with garlic,
packed in crocks, a kind of Tollund butter.

Those odd firkins lost in peat swamps
are now a fossil butter— outside a half-made
sedimentary rock inside the centre's still soft.

Egg Opus

'Eggs are all they're cracked up to be.'

Attrition sees off most

Starting off my life as an egg, I wait
24 years, give or take a cycle, jostling
through the other two million oocytes
who drop like flies, to make an ova.

Nomenclatures

For quite some years I called
my sister Megan Omelette.

Edgecliff, Great Thorn Street, Saturday

We find the bantam's stash
of twenty eggs, age indeterminate,
pungent with possibilities. Walk
out to New South Head Road
to pitch them into the hiatus
of the railway's vast ditch.
Is this the loss of innocence?

Terms and Conditions

Coddled eggling, that odd term
of endearment, a currency we ran
until the state of us curdled.

Six Hour Eggs

I follow interstate, arrive to a kitchen empty
but for a kettle and two plates; a hundred glass jars
on the bedroom floor filled with roses.
I decide to boil eggs in the kettle for salad nicoise.

Summer beckons, a smooth drive
to the wineries. At McLaren Vale
I recollect I left the eggs on.

Decide that nothing can be done, proceed
heedlessly. Manage even to forget them.
On my return I find the water's gone,

the eggs are brown, stuck and seething
with a pulsing hiss, like a cat cornered
in a hot spot, the shells open a little

as if to spit, and then seize up.
I turn off the heat and they lie there,
panting.

O! Egge

O Egg that is on loan from the future
O Egg that is poached from chickens
O Egg that boils detective fiction
O Egg that scrambles the past
O Egg that did not tempt Sam
O Egg that went green with ham
O Egg that smartens the head
O Egg that is a benediction
O Egg that walks on shells
O Egg that ranges freely
O Egg that is rotten
O Egg that fries up
O Egg that eggs on
O Egg that is Nog
O Egg that egg sits
O Egg that plants
O Egg that is an O
O Egg

A Vivid Lesson in Caution

It was pikelets, or going to be,
the last of the milk, the final puff
of flour from the packet,
and then the blood red egg,
cracked straight into the bowl.

Wise Cracks

You're teaching three year olds
to crack eggs, show the measured tap,
the pulling apart, how to work with gravity's
sweet measure, and then watch and learn
how things can go perfectly wrong.

Whisk-full

The whites that lie like slime,
wobble-jelly viscous, cling first
one way, then another,
to the whisk, take on airs,
impersonating rococo clouds,
winding up baroque-en hearted.

Curatorial Eggs

The curate — that great pragmatist —
married to the church, knew
that's always how marriage works.

Miss-carriage I

She's ten in a grey cotton uniform
short sleeves angled up her skinny arms
by a dress-maker's economising scissors,

a pocket at the hip holds the cake-day egg,
warmed in its second nest,
she slaps to signal satisfaction at its presence
smashing it into an unanticipated birth,

egg albumen and yolk running through
the grey cloth and down her leg.

Her cousin, same height and weight,
is pleased to deal with accidents of exuberance,
takes her home, re-dresses her in her grey cotton
puts a new egg in her small hand.

Miscarriage II

Cleaning up, a shift and in the sink,
— my heart likewise— a dark gout
and though the years have slipped past
pegged and un-pegged from the calendar
with the rest of us laughing, adamant
haranguing, well, living I would say

can I call you you? because although
at first reluctant, for three months
you were you for me and my body was
home to you and in that quiet sense
of each, you trusted me completely

back then your dark stains of wasted protein
held my throat so tight I could not think
to say goodbye.

Barn Marbles

Eggy weggs, cackleberries, huevos,
eggliones, chook fruit, googs,
uovo, oeuf, ovo, scramblers,
free-rangers, Veggs, laid-to-order,
dozeners, yolkdoms, two-tone fruit,
marble caskets, begs-the-question,
chicken slugs and poultry pills.

Buffoons of the food world

The egg is the great fall guy,
exemplar of what can't be undone
like words that don't unsay themselves.
Take Mr Dumpty's sorry mess, a knock down
kind of argument, as he might digress
for the Egg to be more or less remastered
—language being what you choose—
but the King's men and their horses
are not up to it and quite remorseless.
Better bet is Alice and her line
of inquisition regarding glory.

Over Easy

First you feel those discreet nudges,
a slight sideways sliding then,
the world tilts alarmingly
and whoosh, you're flat on your face,
believe me nothing is over easy.

Oblate Ovoid's Structural Properties

Pushed polar-wise
the egg shell won't tell a soul
refusing to divulge its contents
but squeezed about its equator,
says yolk to shell,
see you later.

Ova-tures

The corpus luteum sets
up that crampy song
with the chorus line
it's ova, it's ova.

How to Make Powdered Eggs

Take as many as is needed,
a swansdown puff
and talc, proceed, *ad lib.*

Egg-Beaters

Gear ratio that goes
nowhere fast
whirring into eggs
et al.

Nest Eggs Superannuated

Too many eggs in the basket
are needed before you get
into the casket.

Egglogue
Death hatches from fertile eggs.

Mulberries

(Written on the occasion of seeing dried white mulberries in Shaza's Persian Groceries.)

Somewhere I am in a mulberry tree,
tucked into the green skirt that nearly drapes
the ground. I am wearing blue shorts
and a white top, a two-piece set made
of terry-towelling, and on the top, appliquéd,
are green leaves and under this a calyx suspending,
free, terry-towelling strawberries, that are delicious
but inedible and then to one side, and then another
splatters of dark mulberry juice, indelible.

Spice Trader

Your amalgam, a pestling of hard seeds
and dry leaf, has vanilla moments
not plain but sweet, tempered down with constant
coriandering, enlivened with words of sumac,
heat of chili on the tongue, the sharp
and pungent turns galangal-ish,
and your barberry tang that raises shiver
from the well below my solar plexus,
shakes up taste buds on my torso, before it sinks
into the sub-continent of spice.

I offer back a citric acid discipline,
the honey bee's diasporas, mycelia of salty plums
that spring backwards from the tongue
what you never thought to think, as day dissolves,
about the ragged illegalities of juniper.
or might you ask, before all the aromatics
do some limbo in ras el hanout, about the rosehips?

More Information to Help You Get to Rookwood

Email Subject Heading from Urban Sketchers

Keep breathing, every breath brings you
closer, eat plenty of fried food, and soft cheese,
sedentarise those still ambulatory parts
of your life, spend time in hospital waiting rooms,

trawl the infectious wards then rub your eyes.
Loiter in seedy alleys, borrow heavily
from hit men, share needles with the IV user crew.
Eat five day old soup fermented in the pot.

Cry a lot. Wear your immune system
on your sleeve, breathe in other people's
sneezes, speed— while texting— in cars
whose brake warning lights are semaphoring.

Cultivate late night snoring, get livid over
pettifoggeries while eschewing beta-blockers,
move to the bottom of the socio-demographic,
eat more meat, insult fundamentalists in print

giving your real name and address, work
night-shifts in a Chinese coal mine, call the police,
assassinate a senior member of a cult, take a pencil,
draw a short straw and suck.

Three for Four *Save up to $2.77*

It's ginger beer for sale
at '3 for $5 or 3 for $4'.
Odd the things that don't add up.
The car's now full of petrol
as we take off with '3 for $4'
leaving behind the Caltex Station's StarMart
and Davidson's Bushland Cemetery.
No Learners— the graveyard gate says.
This must be true, there is no learning
to be dead. Still there was
the chance to take up ambiguity's
better offer. Though the cashier
cashiered the '3 for $5 or 3 for $4'
sign from the shelf, I still have photo-
graphic evidence, that there are choices
and we must insist.

Parking backwards at Beauty Point

For Kerry Leves 5 May 2011

I reverse, park parallel but *volta face*
to watch the light, the day, ebb
westward into night. The pins of light
reducing in the distance, colour gone
from all the trees, a flag dances dispirited,
settles against its pole, then picks up again.
Two antennae in silhouette, compass points
to vagaries, bring back the image of his thin hands,
newly flecked with purple, his bones drawing
closer to the surface, death gathering him
in cell by cell, organ by organelle,
closing down pipes, thirst and hunger,
raising the last unruly stand of hair,
fading its rust to grey, while he listens
and smiles in a wide, wild beam of pleasure.
Ok I hear him say, and will again, *You right?*
Let's rock and roll

Owl Service

For Frances Mabel Cotton 1917-2008

Flying back, Melbourne-Sydney, keeping pace
with sunset, we are way above the clouds,
Earth twenty thousand feet below, the horizon sweeps
like the clean gesture of a precise pirouette
balancing two halves, two hemispheres.

I've been in that ersatz sleep of travel,
know I'm travelling but dislocated
I seem to be on a bus from Rushall Park
or the train from Mount Kuring-gai
and wake to watch the grey velvet felt
of clouds below, and to the west
sunset's bravura inversion of the spectrum
the blue as deep as any melancholy
brightens into its own vignette
and there it hugs the mountains
in its contained, ecstatic passion
of carmine, sienna, crimson lake,
a stain of blood, and muddy red
edges slate green earth, which seems so distant—
so improbable we will land,
and then you don't, of course,
you fly on into all atmospheres.

Acknowledgements

Grateful acknowledgement is made to the editors of the following journals, serials, newspapers and anthologies in which some of these poems were first published: *Alba, Alimentum, Antipodes, Australian Fabian News, Azul, Famous Reporter, Mascara, Island, Meanjin, The Merri Creek, Semaphore Dancing: Poetry At The Pub Anthology 2009, Small Wonders, Snorkel, Time with the Sky: Newcastle Poetry Prize Anthology 2010, Wagtail, The Weekend Australian,* and to the judges of the Vera Newsome Poetry Prize. Special thanks to the Australia Council for a grant which enabled and encouraged me to write these poems.

The line 'If weather is the watch, climate is the calendar', on page 54 is taken from the Australian Bureau of Meterology's website.

My thanks to David Musgrave, Ingrid Periz, Michael Sharkey, my Sunday Poetry Group, John Watson, and most importantly, Stephen Nettleton.